AF344668

Middle School Thoughts

Halyn Kramer

BookLeaf Publishing

India | USA | UK

Middle School Thoughts © 2024 Halyn
Kramer

All rights reserved.

No part of this publication may be
reproduced, stored in a retrieval system, or
transmitted, in any form or by any means,
electronic, mechanical, photocopying,
recording or otherwise, without the prior
written permission of the presenters.

Halyn Kramer asserts the moral right to be
identified as author of this work.

Presentation by *BookLeaf Publishing*

Web: www.bookleafpub.com

E-mail: info@bookleafpub.com

ISBN: 9789360944759

First edition 2024

To my loving little brother, Teddy. May God bless you with plenty of love and laughter as you walk the path of life. And I am so glad you are joining our family permanently!

ACKNOWLEDGEMENT

I would like to acknowledge the people in my life who gave me encouragement and a reason to keep writing, including my Language Art teachers Mrs. Tabor and Mrs. Baucum. And to Mrs. Hazle who expanded my world of poetry and gave me more confidence in myself.

And a thank you to my family for making and shaping me into who I am today. I love you guys so much, even though it sometimes doesn't look like it. And a special thanks to my mother who helped finance my dreams after a lot (and I mean a lot) of nagging.

And of course a section for all of my besties and classmates. I have to say, they have given me must of my inspiration. I want to give a shout-out to all my very best peeps in the whole wide world; Jordyn Ammons, Lily Baucum, Brylee Blankenship, Kendall Crew, Margaret Dunn, Rhett Edlin, Ash Gibbs, Justice Graham, Kaylee Heater, Olivia Ingram, Reagan Kaster, J'li Lyons, Eden Lutz, Alexis Pfohl, Gracie Rager, and all those other people in my life!

I also want to add for those who tried to tear me down in life. Guess what, it didn't work, and I am still here and stronger than ever! Those people only helped me to become wiser and better, along with a lot of inspiration! I didn't let you win then, and I won't let you win now, no matter how hard you may try.

And to my readers. I love you so much for giving me a chance to make it in this world of poetry and writing. I am honored that you guys decided to pick up this book and read it. Thank you so much!!

PREFACE

This book is about my wonders and thoughts as I finish middle school and get ready to take on high school. It is a collection of my fears and my loves, my ups and downs throughout my time in middle school especially as I work on and struggle through my relationships with God and those around me.

Immortal

A tree standing all alone.
Tougher than metal,
stronger then bone.
The bark unbreakable.

Bright green leaves,
with spots of pink blossoms.
Her favorite thing to do was
to gather and toss them.

Twirling in the falling petals,
wearing a white cotton dress.
Her spirit will never settle.
Immortally lively and lovely.

My Mind

Grey walls surround me.
They are covered with decorations,
that are meant to make it "cheerful."
A person stands at one wall and talks.

The person drones on and on.
And I slip further and further away.
I have no interest at all.
My mind is elsewhere.

It has its own little world.
My mind has become my refuge.
My cozy little safe house.
No one else is allowed in.

My mind creates beautiful azul skies
and grasses that smells like dirt and
chocolate at the same time.
It creates an amazing odor.

Trees stand tall and stubborn.
Oceans gleam beneath the golden sun.
Exotic animals all around.
They are brave and healthy.

I get lost in my mind.
But that's not a bad thing.
It is a pure blessing.
I feel at peace for once.

Worries fade away and-
RING! RING! RING!!
I am jerked back to reality.
To the grey walls and wooden desks.

I stand up with the others
and walk toward the door, fully awake.
I am away from my mind's haven.
But I will be back soon.

Everything, Anything, Something

Everything
That's what I want to be
That's what I want to do
It's everything.

Anything
That's what I want to be
That's what I want to do
It's anything.

Something
That's what I want to be
That's what I want to do
It's something

I want to be worth everything
I want to be worth anything
I want to be worth something
Because it is better than nothing.

Shameless People

I sometimes wish
I could hide
from my mistakes
I still feel guilty about.

Even when I am forgiven.
When the mistake happened
a very long time ago.
When they may not remember.

I still remember though.
When I lay awake at night,
it all comes back to me
and a wave of guilt washes over.

It is always mixed with shame,
because I am also embarrassed
myself when I made that mistake.
It all builds up in my chest.

Sometimes I wonder if others
feel shame like me.
Because if they do,
I have never noticed.

Or perhaps they hide it
because they want to
appear unfazed or
unforgivable.

I am not proud of my mistakes
or the shame and guilt I
feel because of them.
I am proud to act and be human

Those who have no shame
are not human.
They will never be human.

Who Will Be A Hero?

Why can't I be a legend?
Why can't I be known everywhere?
Maybe I can start a civil rights organization,
solve world hunger or poverty.

Maybe stand up against
a terrorist group like Malala.
Or save a child from
a burning building like in the movies.

But those people that did
those heroic deeds were brave.
And I am not and will never
be brave and heroic.

I am a coward.
I am not proud it of,
but I know that I am one.
I will embrace that fact.

I will walk by
a person on the ground.
A suffering person
without reaching out my hand.

Sometimes I wonder if
I can't reach out my own hand,
who would reach out a hand
for me, when I fall?

Will there be someone
to help me up?
Or are we all cowards?
Is there no such things as heroes?

I know that
I should practice
what I preach.
I should do what I say.

But I don't have the guts or grits to.
So I am telling you to be a hero.
Extend your hand.
Build up your courage.

Because if you don't become a hero,
Who will?

I Will Still Scream Louder

Silence is never quite silent.
Nothing is silent.
The air is always whooshing.
The earth is always moving.

You can stuff earmuffs
over my ears.
But I will still hear
the thoughts in my head.

Even if everyone went deaf,
there still would be sound.
I will throw back my head,
and I will still scream louder.

Birds will still sing.
Plants will still rustle
in the passing wind.
Leaves will still crunch underfoot.

There are so many sounds.
Some we are familiar with,
others we don't even
have names for.

You can't silence the world.
We will never be quiet.
Try to shut me up,
and I will only scream louder.

Demons will still cackle.
Angels will still play their harps.
God will still look at you in your eyes
and tell you He loves you.

The world will never be silent.
No matter how hard you try.
No matter how many people
you cut down and kill.

Sound will still appear.
You can't fight it.
Release the silence you hold
and let the sound wash over.

It will cleanse you.
And I will still scream louder.

I See Both

11

What unites us?
Is it love?
Is it hate?
I look around
and see both.

Strings Of Truth

Truths are strings.
They are made of
spider-silk and thread,
ribbon and twine.

The ugly truths
are made of
coarse rope that
rubs and catches
on your skin.

Honesty is a forest
of string; of truths.
Both the pretty
and the ugly.

A tranquil forest
living in perfect
harmony.
Until you come in.

You are bulldozer.
You snap the
pretty strings,
leaving the ugly ones.

You break them
and then you
knot them
with lies.

The forest of
honesty is no more.
No more harmony.
No more pretty strings.
Just ugly truths
and lies.

Cure For My Thoughts

Thoughts flash through my head.
One by one, or two by two.
There is no order, no schedule.
It just jumps from one to another.

Thoughts are happening in my brain
at this very second, this very moment.
I even think at night, when I sleep.
Through all my restless dreams.

I am thinking about a book I've read,
the way the sky looks or my reflection.
What someone has said or is saying,
what I am putting in this poem.

I am thinking about who hates me
who loves me or likes me.
Or who I myself hate or love.
Sometimes I think about perfection.

I think of what would happen
if I was perfect, if I did everything
absolutely, exactly right.
If I got everything I've ever dreamed of.

But my thoughts tell me that it is
not going to happen at all.
Someone else gets it, no matter
how hard I try and practice.

I try to say no, to say no
to my thoughts, but they twist
everything to fit their perspective.
There is nothing I can do.

Just let my know when you find
the cure for my thoughts.

Freedom

Sitting on the bus,
feeling each bump in the road.
Kids being quiet and alone.
Others screaming loudly.

I watch the white clouds. They
are swiftly moving, without stopping.
So unlike the bus.
Not weighed down with anything.

I watch a small bird.
Watched it dip and rise.
It spread out its wings
and took to the blue skies.

I wished to follow it
further and further away.
All it left me was this poem
And a longing for true freedom.

Why? Just Because

Why?
Why do we send perfectly good,
perfectly whole people to die?
Why?

Why?
Why are we so happy during life,
knowing that death is always coming?
Why?

Why?
Why do we fall, and still get up?
Knowing that we must fall again?
Why?

Why?
Why are we here?
Why do we live?
Why?

Maybe just because,
just because we have to.
Just because we want to.
Just because we know love is greater.
Because we know love is better.
Because we know love is stronger.

A Description of God

I can't describe him, because anything
I say about him would be lie.
For words do not describe The Lord Almighty.
They do not describe His power and love.

They are not enough.

Nothing is Something

Nothing is nothing.
That's what they say.
But I believe that
nothing does not exist.

There is a word that
describes "nothing".
It is not nothing
if it has a description.

When I say "nothing"
many may think
of empty air
of something invisible.

But just because you can't
see it doesn't mean
that it is not there.
Because there is something.

Nothing is always Something.

Oh, Lord, Love

The door swung open silently
and revealed a horror.
She stood there in black
with a knife shining like armor

held in her pale hand.
It was positioned over her heart.
I realized what she was doing
and I knew my part.

My feet carried me to her.
My hand knocked the knife out of the way.
She turned to me with empty eyes.
Eyes that were a thousand light-years away.

Eyes that held no love.
Nor any joy, like a shut door.
My arms embraced her
and we sank to the floor.

And we cried.
Tears filled our eyes.
Wrenching sobs shook our bodies,
for she nearly left, nearly said her goodbyes.

If not for me, she nearly said farewell.
I pulled her from the brink of death,
from the brink of hell.
She buried her face deep,

deep, deep into my hair.
Tears ran down my neck.
But I didn't care
for I held on all the tighter.

She had witnessed no love
not until this moment.
She was just someone to push and shove,
until I held her with care.

Love, powerful love.
Love, strong love.
Love, moving mountains love.
Love, fateful love.

Oh, Lord, love.

Made Of

The moon is made
of silver.

The sun is made
of gold.

The earth is made
of emeralds.

The oceans are made
of sapphire.

We are made
of dirt.

Ashamed

Another fight.
Another round
that I had
to witness.

More screaming
more blame.
When will it stop?
Who will go over the edge?

I am sorry to say this,
but I am ashamed of you.

I Wish I Could Say

24

You say,
"Come to me."
I wish I
could say,
"I tried."

I step close
to reach out
with my hand.
But when our
fingers touch,

I break away,
hurting.
Back to my
previous sins
and treason.

I wish I
could say,
"I'm sorry."

Too Far

Another night
where I cried.
Another rumor
you threw among them.

Why?
After everything
we have been
through? All those years?

I remember us
trying to get seats
next to each other
on the bus.

How we joked
and laughed.
I only became aware
of your true self later.

I stood to the side
as you tore down others
with your sickening
gossip and lies.

I watched as you
ran out of people
to hurt. How you
turned to your friends, claws ready.

You made me choose
between you and
my real friends. How
I hated that and how I worried.

Then it was the
final straw. You
had done it officially.
I said my goodbyes.

How done I was.
I realized your real intentions,
how you made everything
about you.

You had gone
too far down
the path of sin
and hurt.

I thought we
were done
with each other.
Until that day.

It reached my ears
that you had
the final laugh.
Calling me such a foul name.

You had teamed up.
And decided to hurt me
even more, with someone
who doesn't even know me.

Do you not
remember how I
stood up for you
and stuck at your side.

I thought we were
equal, until I had
to scrape you off
like some mold.

I was free.
Some days I slightly
missed you. So
I waited.

I waited for you
to say the words
"I'm sorry,"

so I could forgive you.

I never expected
that lowliness to
come from you. I always imagined
someone else would say it.

Good luck
getting my forgiveness
now. You would have
to grovel before me first.

"Some friend,"
I think. Some loyalty.
I wonder, what made
you so bitter

that you swiped
out at me?
You forget how
stubborn I am.

How I don't take
that kind of crap
from a person
such as you.

I am warning
others now.

That if a friend follows
and worships

the sins of gossiping
and spreading rumor,
fix their ways. Lead
them away.

Stop standing
and watching
the victims before
you become one too.

And the person this poem
is about, remember this too.
Quit hurting others just because
you may be pained.

Waves

The music
comes in waves
like a green sea

It sweeps you
off your feet
and makes you lost.

But it will be fine,
surrounded by sound
with different meanings.

One step
then another one
And you become one

Each footfall
is a note
that sways away

Spin slowly
Feel its form
Feel the emotions

Sob your heart out
while laughing
and dying

and flying
and twirling
and leaping

and hurting
and falling
and loving

For music
always
comes
in
waves

My Definitions

Bravery
Bravery is
the ability to do
something no one else will.

Courage
Courage is
being strong enough
to push through the frightening.

Love
Love is
wanting and needing
holding and protecting something dear.

Nature
Nature is
the raw form
of perfect beauty.

Humanity
Humanity is
disgusting, too powerful,
too stupid, too wrong, too evil.

This are my definitions.